TRANSPARENCIES
LIFTED FROM NOON

CHRIS GLOMSKI

MEETING EYES BINDERY

Acknowledgements:

Grateful acknowledgement is made to the editors of the
following publications in which some of these poems first
appeared or are forthcoming: Notre Dame Review, The
Octopus, parlorgames, Pom2, and sidereality. IL LA
appeared first as a chapbook from Noemi Press.

The author would like to express his gratitude and
thanks to: Michael Anania for his kindness and friend-
ship. Jeff Clark for his exhortations. Sharon P. Holland for
her support and assistance in bringing this book to press.

Thanks also to my parents.

Library of Congress Cataloging-in-Publication Data

Glomski, Chris, 1965-
Transparencies lifted from noon / Chris Glomski.
p. cm.
ISBN-13: 978-0-923389-70-3
ISBN-10: 0-923389-70-9
I. Title.
PS3607.L66T73 2005
811'.6--dc22
2005016855

CONTENTS

To Jennifer

IL LA

Ognuno sta solo sul cuor della terra...

—SALVATORE QUASIMODO

First the flash, then the thunder.

                                    Lying talking in bed about the rain

                    "I love the rain"

"And the sun makes me happy"

                    And the sun is hiding in the rain

"As you are hiding in your eyes"   *Why do you say that?*

                              Details, an uncle who called his wife "Raine"

What we're willing to say:

"Can we talk about something else now?"

                    Because it goes like   going back a little at a

time

a day, a year, a day   to be free of it   it goes

like

First the flash, then the thunder

"Look closely at my language," Francesca Vigna said,

"il vetro, the masculine *glass,* goes inside *la finestra,* the feminine *window,"*:

dark-eyed, southern
Francesca Vigna

in inglese:
Frances Vine

Sitting staring through a window,
hours into rain that was
repeating

   "while raining, it rains."

Water

drips

in one of the apartments, a motor rasps
and recedes.
It is dusk all day in via della Faggiola, 12.
As in the old film effect, the one in which the clock
hands swim round the dial through a cross-eyed lens,
this day winds by each window of the house. First
the street at noon, men pulling their huge straw
brooms like oars, packs of schoolchildren, day-glo
knapsacks bobbing behind them as they maneuver toward
              the Leaning Tower.
Enter the washed light of my room, the ivy breathes
on the walls outside. Then the street again at mid-afternoon,
deserted, an occasional voice, a footfall, wind.
When the real hour of dusk has finally swung round,
between two of the bars on my window a strand
of cobweb vibrates, is stretched back like a bow, then sags again;
it doesn't break. Nothing has changed: nothing
has stopped changing.

                        On the Lungarno, her fuck-all stride, tossing all that
hair,
                              *ciao*ing a stranger, Francesca, her vine.

when they turn

I know there must be some truth there,

                  for so many to see something *in me*

                        it must be there,

it's how I know my—

"I hafta meet my pusher in the piazza dei miracoli."

Through a window:
Blue Line train, morning, January, Monday

Chicago
Ci cago

through

                        headlights rushing from
an overpass and dopplering by the guard-rails

Chain-link rust

                              & faces
                              on the platform
                              full of winter

                              "Addison will be next"

Tires flinging up ice

                              bulbs in sequence
                              across a marquee

1 (800) COLLISION

                              What was

through the little window
I have to you, the glass?

A CLEAR DAY IS HERE

the you the

Water tank sky
Starling struck

SIDNEY SHELDON: NOTHING LASTS FOREVER

The life paint of your face's grip on you,
the paint of the life of a face—-

almost illegible, only

First a flash

in a supermarket, winter sun through storefront
lays glow on
a mesh of oranges being scanned, oranges held in a woman's hands & how

dizzy with   *What you*

dragged   a little, back, like through a window,

                              Until   again

June, morning, the day's hot forecast
trudging through screens into bedroom

                                        to be

beaten into breezes by ceiling fan into whose
whirling blades my thoughts on green sheets tumbled:

dumb joy of an oldies station straining under your unconscious sing-along,

smoothing your clothes with an iron warm as the day would nearly be

the room is you
                        smoothing your shirt
and you and the song

                        rolling green within the walls

                                    & outside the supermarket carrying
the oranges
tires flinging up ice

everyone is alone
in their car
on the heart

                                    of thunder

a flash becomes

When in the morning sun-up strikes a kitchen,

haloes whole window above sink, bringing out the full

yellow brilliance in a bottle of dish soap

whose label reports

If Dawn gets in

your eyes, rinse

with water

Fuel

once I heard a hollow thump
        a stair being climbed inside me

Clair de Lune

Your eye light's
conquesting
motion of
contested moons
all gaiety
in leap year's rud rose
fuming   Fine fine
flutter wing stream
goldenly golden seam, lie
still behind this door

*   *   *

The bed your hair
lit shivering   The ball
all *Clair de Lune*
and dissonance
Languid yellow holster
languid arc
in orange arm sleep,
talk taking
tick in it in
this you are
familiar

The Width of a Circle

I am primed to smoke fun in the floral houses, tattooed
       as they are to the prism of my eye.
            There they do not erupt in courtesies,
because their light is tended by fusuma refractions
       which enter my mind whenever I'm driving.
           They are vegetal, a twitch in slumber,
alive outside though unidentified, neither post nor meadow,
       or they are tapedeck and plangent and driven by refrigerants.
           Chewy and loose on the inside. The rearview
garners an extent I've discovered, your face's x-ray vision.
       The long article said "innominate bone…could not…inosculate,
           resulting inquietude……..becoming insalubrious"—
though *in situ* I still feel my core glance insatiably,
       as if innervated by hailstones tearing through arbors,
           where ringing words swell circles inside me.

Willows of Moonlight

Once I thought I heard a hollow thump,
      a stair being climbed inside me
and a sea-serpent broke, in slaps
      of waves as in a sacrament, over me—

It arose and it ended. Freely feeling
      rumors bound the brusque chapel
in calligraphic speech,
      scratching a deep channel bridged only

occasionally by a slovenly moonlight
      and what the willows were thinking

Automatic Control

Chokehold of their missing arms,
Daylit and watched by what you wanted, there by serene incinerators,
One out of seven claims on your louse-packaged heart.
I detest that mendicant lake
The tarnished sun-motes filter comment upon, a shore her steps have
                                          not divided.

To see me handled
By my errors, catching and throwing a rubber ball.
When I stepped out to say what bothers,
Everywhere our terrible hair thinking
Me   You   Him
Like a strange infusion of paper lanterns and movies.
Flailing its tree-like arms a tree torn
Into is place and part of the arbor. The stormy and loud inventions
Chew right through themselves. Parts eaten
Force a glimpse of the hair of a field
Tangled and brown and green. Lately, lately.
No one walks that fence, though it
Is fully in us, severe in being elsewhere not at all.

Song

Paris wick kibble bed, harrow eat moon
   matchstick jai alai starving a cry
   cough granny halo plan mal granny sigh
Melting god ice cream El Salvador womb

Cry bye sponge on cream everlasting
   word spurt starve fur reticular thrills
   China wall painted by us on pills
No more cure for that kind of fasting

Cement hour pome shoes hillbilly shill
   euphonic emergency to screech i'th'sky
   sand is good eye in weir dice testing
Bloody lost bank account, bye Cameroon

Conversing with Eyedroppers

You and the other riders, post-communion
post-wandering-space, violet tendrils teasing
holes in your ontological pockets. A bird's eye
freezes my mind, inducing vocal chords to seize
inside a new you, new planets to sway inside a spit-shine.
NO BREATH ALLOWED is stuck in reservoir gravel,
implying suicide as a notion of down-time, as bloodied tube socks
with burn-holes wind their way toward you in serous water
and you are bitten when you place your hand in one and gag. Buildings
slather shadows, evening on the Nile of Lies. That helium
around hilltops, is it finally behind you? One dithers, wishing for Li Po
                                        suction when
the moon sneezes in one's eye, dropletting silver anchors.
Soft pea breath whispers, "You'll
never need another mattress dealer," and in the calendar
all twelve pictures stand for colored numbers.

Tomato Zulu undid my seventh fork porch,
which, prematurely tweaked, made taint in Helen's grave.
So we booed while sooth was yearning, we
sued while youths were burrowing into "The Heart without Café Stairs."
An iron ember burned through burgundy. The farm eclipsed
our resemblance to nomadic colonies. We carded a woolly
shadow-bike, and made up questions regarding the Seer who
smoked so that lavender engrossed him. Trick fen slurps cracked lung
                                        umbrellas, then,
in flight over a loam-tree's distant Halloween,
in transparencies lifted from noon, the tan sprocket lactated.

It Wants to Go to Bed with Us

A laundromat. That suited, halted man, halted
but smiling——   who eased into, then
backed off, street. His hat. Zoom. Hangers.

This must be the beginning of the great disappointments,
perspiring and dolorous, mean
as meaningless twilight. Who basks

between our ears? Meaning you.
Dying, eh? (In the end there is, uh, the end.) Cinders
in the eye, piecemeal, it was. Are you relaxed?

Hair tosses. We are mostly leaving,
slantways, doorways, going like evening into a lake.
Sounding the blood into night.

Kept stopping for a while, like if I'd forgotten, but that

shirt's done. It's done, and I won't take it with me.

Vela (The Amanuensis)

Concerning the disappearance
one spring of Vela, the amanuensis, I was meditating
not for the first time on these verses, which apparently she'd left
behind

in her Selectric on the desk:

"Thunder of sprung weather!
Rolling like one fallen
down campanile
stairs, or like a moonlash across
that column where
heaves *Abundance* by Pierino
da Vinci, season of lessons
in lightning the palace walls
remember. Now, these many
years later, this window-
fan whirls as of a domain
in those nights, as if
a little rain still dried
on your mosquito
netting. Recalling a piano's
way of enthralling you,
eating fragrant ham
and melon, your eyes
fluttered like *send help*
scrawled on bedsheets, which my
fright stowed then in a basket
of unbelievable indifference.
That *tramonto* seemed
determined to scoop
out all the others. A pane's
spontaneous combustion,
an effigy of ourselves on fire,
and the later appraisals
descried in cooler stares.

Wriggling perfumes, the
avenues of taxis. Shall innocence
invent a vandal
to unplank the undertaker's
fence, the one he
erected one soft October?
A way to exist, our part
in distance, though of a piece
with feelers, deranged by strophes..."

At this point the curtains
beside me began a violent writhing, and something electric
tore out the text and sucked it into the weather. Only on
closer inspection some days later did I find, still stuck
in the carriage, a little bottom-scrap of paper:
"for half of night's a gale," it read, "and you are sailing."

Lights of Other Days

We could say "Afternoon dreaming me, a typical Sunday."
As far apart from other days as we are by them enclosed.
Sun-touched walls. Shining blankly where you stood folding towels
in the south room into which shadows squeezed. A distance.
Who imagined this might be taking place in some book?
Sills inhaled curtains, which collapsed, sleeping.
"Coming out of me, living is thinking." "And thinking, sleeping."
An imperfectly practiced aimlessness on Sundays,
until all was like evening falling open, apart. A random page in a book.
Spilling out like some old mimeograph a child had enclosed.
Growing large hands from those lost to the distance.
Strange frolic of fright again, as in a dark closet full of towels!
You write, "When I come to visit, should I bring toothpaste, towels?
Do I arrive at some hour that typically finds you sleeping?
What are the teeth within the stretched distance
between us? Do they impose on your being like Sunday's
liturgy, which a seventh part of our youth enclosed?
Fogged over, as in the cellophane of prayer books?
Is that how you vanished from every phone book?"
Your letter arriving in a heat wave. Wrapped in damp towels,
I handled the little origami boat of happiness enclosed
and in so doing I felt caught up in a dreamy logic of sleeping.
Friday was Thursday was Monday was Sunday.
The hours staggered out of their immense distance
and entered us, installing each other's absence, which was distance.
Something gave little more than something. By the book.
The throbbing in whose forehead announces, "It's Sunday
inside that sky, long hung with wet dark towels."
Swept from a high ledge. The falling dream, or the end of sleeping?
Again moving among things your dream had enclosed.
Its secrets, the meanings of which are seldom, if ever, enclosed.
In my picture of you, your expression is caught up in distance.
Though your eyes are open, you appear to be sleeping.
Shall I ever freely decipher their book?

These buildings. Sandy impressions. Paper towels.
Sunday looks through us right into next Sunday.
You were close in the towels; you were enclosed.
Re-enter the distance. Redouble the Sundays.
We are as we are in no one's book. We may be sleeping.

Her Travels

You don't travel light...

Winds encroach, whistle honeycombed
      in a jerk—sits her up in bed
            Words to her insides join
Fixed in a kiss that kisses
      desert breezes, her branch over current
            stretched—reaching the arm, sleep
tearing everything apart—of a million
      names on doorbells, double-clicking
            All those places, at once on the plain
of a mountainous sea, minute-hand her shadow
      Scrolling through, clicking back
            Who would she be plunging into river,
in her glass it moves; when it's moving
      her same breeze, northern, colder
            Flashcubed into years
red eyes the hot frost snapped
      Descent quickening
            Her floor of one mind, her rails
              when the freight came

FIRE TRUCK ON FIRE

Neither can devil nor hell now appal me—

—-FAUST

dependent on the finite gifts
of a hostile environment

to survive flashes of identity
caracoles, corpuscles

Quietly someone
                    below no one's eye

                                        bleeding in an attic

They hold a tuning fork to his temple:

in a cloud as white as a wing it winks
upon the screen he is dreaming

Paper cut, symptom—

                    "From Ghost"

in a secret scent no one could decipher
  or wouldn't though they well might
whisper it on

   where
simoon or peesash   khamsim or tramontana

               (lurking in wingèd boy-heels)

                        could bear it to one who'd
thrash the thread you are—the thread and it

     a tad raveled

THE PROUD JUNIPERS

Now under cover of their own growth behind the house, now within
the recesses of a bedroom mirror into which they stared, the junipers
were becoming prouder—especially when damp gusts pounded them
against glass and got their greenness reeling. How they thrilled to
their own swayings. Their roots burrowed into earth like words in
membranes. What were they though, these junipers, and who made its
way within them?

its pavid range
lengthened

TOTIPOTENT

We were wandering in flames we were
worshipping as martyrs as the loudspeaker
we heard as a flower required.
Death was an appellation and a spell. We
grew totipotent beneath it. The east
was freaked and it teased with Mayan
writing. We furrowed a stricken plain,
believing grief would seed its ear.
The studio filled with our illness.
A canvas had been thinking
and we chanted, afraid to ask. It was white by
fathoms, a swaying alien, a stray.
It seemed to fight inside us.

Spring is in the air. Row after row of trees, buildings. I think I can feel the sky folding over the sun like a compact. From a tiny opening at the end of the hall, a procession of two advances. My new mother! And my new face is on display in the contours of her chrome chair. My lips swell and simper; I have a cruel, intrusive beak, immense and full of these new odors.

Backward through the temple of another wisdom
                                        should rise
a sentence beyond thinking's finding—
                            then yield
to abuses where *must* is blind

Trees feed the dusts short idylls where
time's double vision shuffles all
into long lines
                    and welters,   giving
                                        your secret a form
to over-ride others   yet to remain
the same blessing one begged of sensations
in falling, though whose blessing is
indeterminable, by feeling or blind calling

        so sensations of change so

    falling

A single garment and yet separate, the wind as it swallows. To this end, in sallies of fear, my own poles couldn't know me. Outside, the lie of the land. It says "the head holds an attic, yet it's ahead of and above me." So I is the lie and this is the land. The bread as it crumbles, the crumbs as they fall, leaves, improvisations of starving.

VIGILS OF THE FIRE

Circle burns, waiting for someone to come
Garden of tucked sleeves, spore finding his
eye; embryos tear lashes from sparks
                                        in a womb

                blasphemous phosphene
                    vacancy   Think it is real

Awake something wicked, in formaldehyde—
                vigils of the fire, totem named Shantih

orders your glass face   eroded by a mistress

who's been in the fire
and sucks red coal   the vigil is as even
                                as fire—it is parity

Could you not stay awake one hour?

                        Skirting open-ended
florally, loathe to whitewash being
as plucked inward there came challenges to flowers
    Something reeling carried itself to couch,
        shrank before new views, then couldn't
        get up

unless down shook trees' to new shushing
for what something might be about

as sudden a vigil by style as danger involved to alter

the red sentence burning is certainly about, its phrase
a fire pushing into the gym, a balance that takes in
a whole world until scale is a vigil by
        fire inside you

OTHER THINGS

...things will light the torch for other things.

—LUCRETIUS

The Blue Shades

A room the color of a sore throat. Very cold. Chirping birds, intermittent thuds, as of falling bodies.

2 shades, Spider & Ivy.

Spider: Three, three, one, eight, zero.

Ivy: It had been uncaged. Alone in the ranch house. Remembering the wall blackened around a phone.

Spider: What's it thinking?

Ivy: Behind bushes.

Spider: Little ones calling from carpets?

Ivy: That is the poverty of its imagination.

Spider: A rock behind some garbage cans.

Ivy: We had lights that could be seen from our sickbeds.

Spider: Seven, as I remember. Do you see wings trembling in a web?

Ivy: We do.

They are covered with dust.

Currency Exchange

After nap, imprints of bedsheet running up arm. Fluorescence. Carnation oil. Siren fades. Federal Savings Bank. Illusions of speed and dexterity. Step 2 and Step 3. There is meter change beneath the seat. Train throws up sparks. A snow-capped Mount Damavand. Quilt swatch of orange and red flowers on a field of midnight blue. *Inconstitucionalissimamente* the Portuguese for "very unconstitutionally." The predetermined. Auto wreck on rock-show poster. New Dmansis skull shakes human family tree. Cat dozes, switches tail across floorboards. Ngunza, Angola. Citron candle next to Yellow Pages. Sun shines. Cobras spit. Shattered walk barred by sawhorse. Microwave blip. 330 PSI @ 73°F. Exclamations. The price of life. Peas and carrots. While I'm closing gate, dog slams other side of privacy fence, claws rasping the planks. Ringing phone. Religions of the world. Ficus on porch. Distressed loved one. Washer falls from nozzle. Unusual May weather. Compositions *de tête*. CTRL+SHIFT+^ (CARET), *the letter*. Long-grain rice. On table two library books and sixteen-count box of Sony 90 minute audio tapes. Enticed by a baited hook. Mount Fuji, "a spiritual citadel." If you have chimeras, good or bad, we want to hear from you. Three ceiling fans, each whirring. Skeleton photo at feet of mannequin legs atop small bookcase in entranceway to living room. "How long will you have that look on your face?" In salon window, neon scissors. Bake sale. Duct tape. Tongue coating. Seeing the yellow hole, I imagine his dog. *Foie-gras.* Cloth-bound books. A&P. Man prepares to wrestle duck on rock-show poster. Five apples, two oranges. Motorcycle rev. Tavern sign. Joggers along Monroe Harbor. Octagons, white and grey, border rectangles of jade on kitchen linoleum. Lant or mental? Light changes on State Street, bus sprays fumes. Car alarm. The next-to-last Coke. Note written in middle of night reads "sea of danger close her eyes." Sonic crash. Red wine vinegar. The pause before telemarketer hooks up with "Hello?" East Caroline Basin, Pacific Ocean. What rhymes with tandoori? Cat litter on floor. Oboes. Gargoyle incense burner on windowsill of closet. Sailboat in Lake Michigan flies "Dont Tread On Me" flag. Squirrel rummages in planter. Gas leak. President's Choice coffee. Oscillating fan. Borneo's proboscis monkeys. Ice cubes melt in dispenser grate. Physical therapy. Wok, teakettle, saucepan. Old Style Beer lamp. Sun glares off neighboring window at precise angle to reflect through mine, flaring for two minutes in lantern patterns on kitchen wall. Forty-nine minus one. Fear puts phone back in a cradle of narrative. Smooth muscle tissue. Wind ray bites skin. Nasturtiums. Organized youth photo. Lipitor. Italian postage stamp depicting Capo d'Orlando. *The Chicago Sun-Times*. Prince Patrick Island. Red wink of smoke detector. Anthems, motets, cantatas. Domino sugar and Morton's salt. Attention-seeking noise originates in cat. Sensitive fern. Stances on suicide. Catered reception to follow program. Red-tailed airliner enters cumulous. Man asks for post-office change. Cell phone plays tune. What causes these mushrooms to grow in a "fairy ring?" Home team. Antivirus program. The Rainbo Club. Double Door. Phyllis' Musical Inn. Gold Star Bar. Big Horse Lounge. 50 lb. sketchbook, 100 sheets. That being the point. Dodge Dart? or Plymouth Scamp? Candelabra shadow. Hammer blows. Goldfish shower curtain. Parked cars behind condos. The night sky. Smokejumpers. Church steeple. A fixed residence in Catatonia. Word-a-Day calendar. Charlie Tuna lamp. Expressway congestion. Missing landmark. Picture frame singed over oil painted candle flame. Saskatchewan. Dental sign blinks time and temperature. Stuporous ants in dregs of sweetened tea.

Guest

Forgive me my foot. My mind, its moat
and nearly not me. Without forget
beneath unlovely tonnage. My natural body.

What if I should cease along illumined rails,
placid or rapt by chrome medallions,
pissing freely up, enjambing

stars? Meaning the imported arm
is what if I should leave you
in causeway of predicate,

dreaming a pulse that clearly traces
feet and speaks
upon the edge, teetering to believe?

Roman numeral: I or one? Two
by our eleven,
each the other's guess inside.

Death Sample

Impalas   the flightdeck
Hypnotic as the bowls of shining fuel
Naked water wants them
Belly light lifting stranded hair   Balloon
Ate lamplit meat   Up lit
Ourselves
The first time we—   alone
Flagrant on
Black sidewinding
Irritably a snare
Apartments slouching
The sand I am wearing
For a face undulant marks
Lighten scratched pikes
Could the child talk
Invested in purple air
Mountain-activated spaces   the loop
In subtle fog
A partition of one's mind   ONE WAY
Erased and blown from margins
Now that I am up in centrality
Along the shores of my infested vault
Tell them a carnival zooms
Wearing night's thread turbidly   its own way
Toward uncertain ends
One extracts hair   Waves shells
The nimbus clears   her high
Bones custodially forming
Our lack of wheels
Across the lobby   her car keys
The oncoming incision
Twilight mosquitoes
Find in birds Lowering
Into bulrushes   Sprinklers
The mad dash seemed forever leading through

Like scaffolds where dotted helmets
Gray windows returning
To work inside others
Their fresh thoughts not exploit
The child's face   shapes
Itself
She laid the wound barefoot across table
Eyes fell upon it
Fell in planets the TV
Wanting twice the rage   shoreling
Of yawing space   Each wary leg
Descending   The vacant family
Room   Paneling or stacked coasters
Its light baffling the rock
Wrenched late from
Green shadows   dark limp aslant
Raved hoarsely across   hose drops
Pelting no umbrella   Jericho
Terms and conditions   His masterpiece by Zola
Zen it seemed was entrenched in tall plots
Backed by W's — the door
Unopened to where it could properly close
Three great shudders the first year
Where there is no sign   Paved
Feinting busts   first a collar from which
Night flowed in a line   Anywhere lines
Cinched to the pavement
His masterpiece "by night"
She is the county's undoing
But fresh
Uncapped prescriptions neatly the sink
The biting man
Photographs himself beside
Reference numbers developmental
His wife's bathing caused problems
Hanging from exhaust vents
Packaged as stars
Mercantilely a Janus
Among other executives
Sent him the platter should quarrelsome heads

But self-made in a tower for
Shouldering signatories
As far as vomiting in a bucket
Morale questions   the empty carousel
Her brother the strapped launderer
See?
They have rightly built around it
As they take into a terror of sighs
To recombine sphinx-like   the entirety
Each flower enters
Stratus of fealty launching slender
Orthopedics
The staging ground through some love deformed
In arrears   the kid's wand
In other words red
Arresting time by a chimney
Still not   still
Across the lurching practitioner
As in a weed climbing
Leaving tight new faces to glow
Restored long lost   not from Srebrenica
Stone atop a letter   might have skipped
In a glide between turnings of slate
Bolting the rails   dissembled
The approximate so
Inside itself
Winching around face-to-face
In an old   stalagmitic
Trouser mignon
If one surfaces   distant inside
Churning with metaphysics
Cuffed to a lacquered dowel
Broken by animal looks   turnstiles—
Gleaming and numbered in morning
An ancient light of dice   languid in passage
As Bellorussian meadows—the piss
Examines me when no one
Of livid solitude crossing texts
Rolling bread in their daily sleeve
On removal   these distances

Are rubble
Undecided or the players contrive
Pale teeth of weld
Albeit other voices one imagined
To have talked off a ledge
In the paratactic sky
To be almost
In the present words
The pit bull of   engines
                    Flames
The dawn   full of decision
Here is a knock   premium arrows
Sticking reverse instructions
The monitors spill
Integral as sinews   space
The pavement wakes
Thin   keen
Suffering arms to carry no more
Stamina holes reaching bleed
The time we're not far from
Structures tracing the ladle
That is death sampled
Parted curtains
"The way around here"
Silted corrosion
Landing on new names   dangles there
Personal cold insight
Stuck to photographic movement
Smoke rolling dark cloth
Your august longboat's wake
Identically shading the plugged outlet
Repeated   September   the handlebars
Though unextinguished
No ladder or throat

On the Edge of the Ice

a metempsychotic interlude

Action set within a tiny cube which contains 1) the Atlantic ocean 2) some kind of ladder with hands 3) a superstar 4) an Advent calendar

Beaumont descends upon a saucer, wearing a cape.

Beaumont: "My eyes are splinters off the scholiast's chisel,"…these are the guesses destined for your pleasure, and it's as such that mourning may never recur with such clarity and softness. True grace sees itself in anxiety these chimes have dreamed of.

He ascends. Enter 2 shades, Fang & Skank.

Fang: Three, eight, four, four, six, six, two.

Skank: Those aren't instructions I would have hoped for!

Fang: Love is the pastor of this…this moving hand.

Skank: As the Concorde is place-marker in every desert?

Fang: You have run decisive rings around me.

Skank: Well, there's no escaping the fact this was all your idea in the first place.

Fang: Do you speak from the "aye" of your own storm?

Skank: Despite my certainty.

Fang: But don't you, each morning, taxonomize your night-
               mares from your dreams?

Skank: Shall we not say a prayer?

F & S: (*together singing*) Sun-blink circumference, total I and
               nine / A bell's a clock and hollow-point / Sun of ticking
               nigh.

Skank: Aren't we stopping?

Fang: Afraid not. Just thought you'd like to see. I'm sorry, and
               that's about all I'll ever be.

Skank: Lucky for you I've just invented the first housekey!

Their wrists are opened by butterflies.

WHERE MAY IT BE LEADING, THIS LIFE AMONG THE FAMOUS?

IT BEGINS WITH

Harry Volkman, TV weatherman, coming to school to address the third grade. About some fundamentals of meteorology, I presume. So few of us watched the news then; the consensus was that it was irrelevant. Yet here was a man who had stepped right off the screens in our living rooms and into the school lobby, where we gathered in highest expectation. Beside ourselves, really, with the very idea....

"NEWHART"

As a little girl, my youngest sister was a playmate to Jennifer Newhart, daughter of the famous comedian. It happened that the star of the *Bob Newhart Show* had a sister who lived in our suburb, though she was no longer "Newhart," having married a man named Kwan. Now and then, her young niece would come stay with the Kwans, whose economy teemed with eight or more kids. But despite the numbers, every one of little Jennifer's cousins far exceeded her in years.

Lest this child of celebrity suffer loneliness and because my mother and Mrs. Kwan enjoyed a confiding rapport, it was agreed that my sister would spend afternoons at Byrd Hill with Jennifer under the supervision of one of her elder cousins. I remember that among these was a girl named Sheila, and that I thought that was a very beautiful name.

"ME + KENNY HOLTZMAN"

scrawled on back of a square, borderless print, in a cursive style more
prone to loopage than now. Kodak paper of rounded corners. A snap-
shot from Picture Day, Wrigley Field, 1970's. Overcast sky, clock hands
on scoreboard fixed at 12:20. Bowl-cut just barely reaching the pitch-
er's shoulder, who flips camera a good-natured smirk, eyes peering
from shadow of cap-brim. Though expression on my face strains
toward nonchalance, there is tell-tale squint that seems caught in the
act of suppressing some deep and private chaos, as if even then I were
concerned that the future of any given moment might rediscover this
version of me, peering as if from some unseemly locket.

THE POET

The first time I visited New York City, I was fortunate enough to have Thanksgiving with a party that included a very great poet. The food was traditional, and talk brightened with each of the wines. But the great poet ate nothing, drank nothing, and said nothing, staring all the while into the mashed potatoes. Our host had to rouse him, at meal's end, with gentle, persistent reminders to the effect that dinner was over.

One summer, many years later, that image—shell of a face reflected in its empty dinner plate—troubled me vaguely as I walked beneath tall trees in a rain of cicadas.

PRELUDES TO AUGURY

And why not the hedge of geysers the obelisk of hours the smooth scream of clouds the sea's quartered pale green spattered by good-for-nothing birds ...

—AIMÉ CÉSAIRE

To the Day

I would ask that you hold me—if not like spoon to
flame then because I am falling beneath the constant and alien
      and fatal in faces. Hurry up good afternoon.

        Know I am what you are looking for,
          stowed in a hip-pocket as you straddle the nights
     and I wish it were true—I do so much there.
Where satellites carve open a green sky, it is enough to look

to be patted down by all of it, and it's all within me, though you have yet
      to see. Suddenly I'm erupting and how quiet.
        Grip me as you would blade, then cut away
          our proper shapes: your talons, my severed finger—
    then for you to perch there, carry me off.

If It Isn't June

A clairvoyance
cherrybombs ringing in the valley.
What in rhymes of mirror holds a believer
at shadow's length, fresh in a certain green and penetrating dust.

We visited a tree and it loaned us something,

                                        it seemed holy
            to be so lulled.

                        Yet you were climbing...

                        There was
                        indulgence,
                        a sower's motion—

the way your J hooked writing

The tree is jaundiced
if it isn't June.

In a Mantle of Sky

For I am leaning out my eyes, thus deep in the need.
Signing. Unable to parse the bottom.
Refreshed by fire. Most joyous fifteenth swaying.
He He He He He   A stalk.
The nest to the least.
Or the thick winds of a gamy flavor. Muffled drum.
Clear morning.

Vireo.
Utterance to both sexes.
0.70 – they settle frequently. The crisp shaft.
0.71 Poland, where silk tails seldom quiver.
0.72 When caged like pale blue.
"L'rrr, l'rrr" As if fascinated.
To the Pacific   Who Is Mighty

In April. Admirable mimic
He whistles for the dog.
Ripe persimmons, he regales himself.
Has Done Great Things
To the aphids that injure our fruits.
Sound of a Jew's-harp   ensconced
Deep in boughs of pine.

A round heap in about six
Tapeworms
Of a very large triumph.
Chiefly found in beautiful undulations
Of Sentinel grain.
Prolonged V's or 1.12 he would alight there.
For Me Me Me Me Me

Mallarmé's Mirror

My incarnadine thought, haze of a cardtable,
     light of a polis we were shaking in—
a curtain of mist drawn over the shore

        proclaimed "sea-worms aren't faking
        shipwrecks, they are sucking the ore"

and a boom of moonlight threw us over

     "From the privilege of saddles
comes hand to mirror, though now
     mines of untested tiny things strip you
like hills of fire"

        An exhalation halved it,
and it assumed shapes, a cormorant in decomposing
     stages
with silent riots in the eye-holes

          Inside, it was taking something over

strange dozens…blue deer…striations of the heard

Mortmain

The clearest intentions involve nothing
I can see. They are a bush when they mean birds.
The wonder of shaking dead hands,
is it too much? Some things.

I can see they mean a bush, for they are birds,
accelerating, meaningful, propelled by auroras.
Is it too much? Some things
packed in wads of insulation, as if

accelerating, meaningful, propelled by auroras,
they become you in the key of your failing,
packed in wads of insulation. As if
even evening came wrinkled by whether

they become you in the key of your failing,
yet tender in a kind of invisibility.
Uneven evening, wrinkled by weather,
a dimness, a din that appears in the mirror,

yet tender in a kind of invisibility.
I wonder where you are coming from as you fade,
the dimness a din disappearing in the mirror,
the blur of whose face…

I wonder where you are. Coming, you fade
in these glistening emblems, wading through
the blur of whose face?
I remember each thing,

the glistening emblems and the wading through.
The clearest intentions involve nothing
I remember. Each thing
shaking in the wonder of dead hands.

Drinking Bird

We needed a sliced and pinned anatomy of the monument.
Something so that the voting would tickle as it trickled in.
There a *momento* moaned over moraines,
the alarms going look-look. The many stragglers
left the waves still guessing. Look at each one. Looking.
At antinomy. At looking up by licking a finger,
they *so do not need one*.

                          This clearly explained the thing's
                  beak.

                         Rice dessert, icelight
spilling through a crescent essence—is there a more
fragrant mirror? It makes the forms tighter, laces
debased lovers, youthful like fire, thinking them same. But
one is only a moment another thinks it is seeking. That is enough
to empty the square of all but ambulant sunlight caught
embracing a vacant plinth. That is where there might
have been a monument swooping down like a shadowy drink
of terror.
          But there were clouds bumping other clouds, the
day had something stolen from its hour. It was as lost
as it was lower. Everything, meanwhile, was getting fuller.

Wings emblazoned on a give-away glass extended.

Nowhere Again

Eagles were orbiting. It was too early in the year for flies.

Newel
post hi-fi ceramic ladyface. The oak tree dropped acorns around the
can's metal netting. Cigar moss peony succulence wedged in three-in-
one, the glistening shears. Thorny shadow of a rose-wound trellis
tapped by dust and fixed in a windowpane. "Why are you lying there?"
"I am a pilot."

Ants were then destabilizing a nickel-sized spot of earth
outside the Legion of Honor.

*Then you may see the mated pair dash to the
edge of the farm pond to scoop up pellets of mud with their bills. But you
can't make bricks without straw, says the Bible, and so they add straw from
the barn floor, and mixing this with mud, they fashion a nest, in shape like
a big coffee cup, up on the chosen beam in the velvet shadows.*

There was a general chaos in the commissary one never
got completely used to. So apart from Jay Nardiello's trim beard and
gold Italian horn. Though *Sterno* was involved in both places and at
both times, it was more the claustrophobic feeling of being tucked away
beneath the grandstands, the older ladies tending vats of boiling
wieners. Behind these was the beer cooler where Alan was taken away
wearing, as usual, a camouflage jacket. Well, what else? A dirty look for
which we'll never be compensated
stomach   bench   study

grinning between gulps of urchin

melon flame igniting sky

ears singed with taxi-whispers, riff-sparked dervish

ventriloquistically

Sherm Mendoza, lately of the fervid valley, could

see through any dated *Bluebook* to a low-level crisis; his carious Western teeth laden with popcorn saddles, his tongue unconsciously grooming them.

Lilac nipples

The hour the transportation grid was lit. Chevrons on his sleeves, despite a lack of affiliation. He looked things over and ordered the chili. A waitress clicked through channels on the big-screen. Partway through a thought, it seemed the word bursts might complete an inconceivable sentence, then dinner was set steaming before him, and the screen was muted. Citizens shared the knife-like silence.

"Do you hear a helicopter?" "Tell me first what you are doing here."

But what if it *is* raining? Will you ever advise to "think through cedar" or "extrapolate roses"? As one little door opens, another one closes. You'll see me writhing butterflies, splayed in fragrance.

The exit parlaying Butte spirals off 90 in and out of the little polis, corkscrewing, the dew and the past unnoticed, it was raining.

On screen an intellectual appears, seeming to mispronounce "nuclear," but it was hard to tell if this registered with co-author Norman Mailer, for the cameras were hardly on him, suggesting he was unarmed during the taping. Unbeknownst to either of them, on the host's morning walk, the sunny sky had shimmered like raw whites around a yolk and a momentary winedark seizure snatched his heart's pendulum; a fragile arrhythmia nourished equations which together almost spelled out "FATH..."

slow exclamations
mustache-channeled satin

"Ghosts flying out of mother and father's bed."
Words brought by a little Spanish girl in a dream, with colors to hide
them in. Grey tentacles washing a mouth in little more than anthers.
Nuzzling the ferns. Thistly contortions. Where are you going
behind Sun Drugs

                                        becoming then flash-
lit and held in the president's hand during blackouts, two and a half
(firefly) seconds ago

osprey-wing of your plucked brow   light-producing cells
                intricate gaze   scientist diagram
pointing arrow   severed black sparrow
        lightning neck
                contac ball capillary   prim floor so
vivid

signed, the experiment

                        Deep summer. Around 8 the bats would
appear. Watching through barred window caught their flights in its
weir   Hoops rolling air through shadows   Webbed wing-planes and
walkers licking gelato   Allergen drowse   Church of San Frediano
Jousting forever on a bridge   Outright below fiery artifice   aftercloud
orange   pinenut   "Nowhere again," they confided, "nowhere,"

they liked that they had arrived

Poking around the Site of My Disappearance

Music makes me embrace
in it, cleared from night   You opened

Two figures were
behind a manger, shaded
by phases of laughing
The sound a founding in twilight, the picture
a figure in falling where one

fire-filled pigeon
                    rises

                                perfect peregrine

            Germinate the square
            Swordmirth gesture infant tryst
            Dispatch the larval prayer
            O theme park lonesome height

...this broken column where the lizard glides
and the ivy climbs...

—HEBDOMEROS

NOTES

Page 7:
Everyone is alone on the heart of the earth...

Page 23:
The title is Kenneth Koch's quintessential Ashbery line.

Page 29:
From the Harvard Classics edition, P.F. Collier & Son.

Page 37:
The Italian term for "firefighters" is *vigili del fuoco.*

Page 39:
Translated by H. A. J. Munro

Page 55:
Cf. Plato, *Phaedrus* 259b-d.
"SOCRATES: Everyone who loves the Muses should have heard of this. The story goes that the cicadas used to be human beings who lived before the birth of the Muses. When the Muses were born and song was created for the first time, some of the people of that time were so overwhelmed with the pleasure of singing that they forgot to eat or drink; so they died without even realizing it. It is from them that the race of cicadas came into being; and, as a gift from the Muses, they have no need of nourishment once they are born. Instead, they immediately burst into song, without food or drink, until it is time for them to die."

Page 57:
Translated by Clayton Eshelman.

Page 61:
Cf. Mallarmé's letter to Henri Cazalis, May 14, 1867, translated by Bradford Cook:
"As you can see, amusement is quite impossible. And yet how infinitely more impossible it was a few months ago when I struggled with that creature of ancient and evil plumage—God—whom I fortunately defeated and threw to earth. But I had waged that battle on His boney wing, and in a final burst of agony greater than I should have expected from Him, He bore me off again among the Shadows; then victoriously, ecstatically, infinitely, I floated downward until finally one day I looked again in my Venetian mirror and saw the person I had been several months before—the person I had forgotten. I should add—and you must say nothing of this—that the price of my victory is so high that I still need to see myself in this mirror in order to think; and that if it were not in front of me here on the table as I write you, I would become Nothingness again."

Page 62:
Literally "dead hand." Primarily a legal term, but also with the sense in *Webster's* of "the influence of the past regarded as controlling the present."

Page 64:
The italicized text is from *The Rainbow Book of Nature* by Donald Culross Peattie, 1957.

Chris Glomski was born in Colorado in 1965 and raised outside Chicago. After studying at the University of Iowa, he lived and worked for a year in Pisa, Italy before returning to Chicago. He is the author of a chapbook, *IL LA*, published by Noemi Press, and is at work on translations of various contemporary Italian poets. At present he teaches at the University of Illinois at Chicago.

MEETING EYES BINDERY

(an imprint of Spuyten Duyvil)

Infinity Subsections by Mark DuCharme
Lunacies by Ruxandra Cesereanu
Savoir Fear by Charles Borkhuis
Diary of a Clone by Saviana Stanescu
Hidden Death, Hidden Escape by Liviu Georgescu
The Maine Book, Selected Poems of Joe Cardarelli
Edited and with an Introduction by Anselm Hollo
Butterflies by Brane Mozetic
Part of the Design by Laura Wright
Of All the Corners to Forget by Gian Lombardo
Transparencies Lifted from Noon by Chris Glomski
No Wrong Notes by Norman Weinstein
Burial Ship by Nikki Stiller